BOOKS BY JUDITH BARRINGTON

HISTORY AND GEOGRAPHY 1989

TRYING TO BE AN HONEST WOMAN 1985

HISTORY AND GEOGRAPHY

HISTORY *AND* GEOGRAPHY

JUDITH BARRINGTON

THE EIGHTH MOUNTAIN PRESS
PORTLAND · OREGON · 1989

"The Bee Sting", "The Wedding Album" and "Off Season" were originally published in *Prospice*; "History and Geography" in *Spindrift*; "Villanelles for a Drowned Parent" and "Another Quarrel" in *Calapooya Collage;* "Out to Grass" in *Blue Unicorn*; "The Hero" and "Dirty Panes" in *Bay Windows*; "Fortieth Birthday Song" in *Common Lives, Lesbian Lives*; "La Bruja del Sueño" in *Sinister Wisdom*; "The House on the Bluff", "Still Life" and "Letters from Eastern Oregon" in *Northwest Magazine* and "Wilderness, High Tech" in *Tapjoe*.

Grateful acknowledgment is made for permission to quote from:
"The Spirit of Place" by Adrienne Rich, copyright © 1981 by Adrienne Rich, taken from *A Wild Patience Has Taken Me This Far* by Adrienne Rich. Reprinted by permission of the author and W.W. Norton & Company, Inc.
"It is the Lesbian in Us. . ." by Adrienne Rich, copyright © 1979 by W.W. Norton & Company, Inc., taken from *On Lies, Secrets, and Silence* by Adrienne Rich. Reprinted by permission of the author and W.W. Norton & Company, Inc.
"Poem for a Birthday" by Sylvia Plath, copyright © 1960 by Ted Hughes, taken from *The Collected Poems of Sylvia Plath* by Sylvia Plath. Reprinted by permission of Harper & Row Publishers, Inc.

The author wishes to thank the Metropolitan Arts Commission of Portland, Oregon for a grant which supported the writing of some of these poems, and Cottages at Hedgebrook for a residency during which this book was completed.

Library of Congress Cataloging-in-Publication Data
Barrington, Judith, 1944-
    History and geography.
    I. Title
PS3552.A73647H5   1989   811'.54   88-33478
ISBN 0-933377-03-7
ISBN 0-933377-02-9 (pbk.)

The Eighth Mountain Press
624 Southeast 29th Avenue
Portland, Oregon 97214

In memory of

Violet Elizabeth Helene (Lambert) Barrington

and

Reginald Jack Christie Barrington

CONTENTS

PART FOUR:

A Memoir

PART FIVE:

History and Geography

The tests I need to pass are prescribed by the spirits
of place   who understand travel but not amnesia.
                                    —Adrienne Rich

PART ONE

Villanelles for a Drowned Parent

And it came to pass at the end
of forty days, that Noah opened
the window of the ark which he
had made. And he sent forth
a raven…
                    Genesis 8:6

I

What does all this mean for me:
the ship and the rescuers coming too late?
You always said you knew you'd die at sea.

You'd say it casually, drinking tea
refilling my cup, passing a sandwich plate
but what does all this mean for me?

Should I, for instance, hold on steadfastly
to my belief that I can foretell my fate?
You always said you knew you'd die at sea

as if, without doubt, you could foresee
that end to the voyage you knew you'd hate
and what does all this mean, since for me

it's a plane, not a ship, that weakens my knee?
I walk, as to death, through that numbered gate
remembering you said you'd die at sea

and that you did, however reluctantly
as if you already knew the time and date.
So what, I ask, does it mean for me
that you always said you knew you'd die at sea?

II

The telephone is underneath the stairs
in an airless, cluttered cupboard, smelling of wax.
The names go on and on, mostly in pairs.

"Mr. and Mrs....safe" the message declares
when we call each hour for days among the macks
by the telephone underneath the stairs.

The ship's still burning, not a vessel dares
to get in close, they orbit in swelling tracks
while the names go on and on, mostly in pairs:

sodden survivors blinking under the flares—
a few in the bottom of lifeboats, flat on their backs.
The telephone is underneath the stairs

where each of us takes a turn and each of us swears
at the brooms and polish, matches, crayons and tacks,
and names go on and on, mostly in pairs.

One of us watches the news and one of us stares
at impossible newspaper headlines growing in stacks.
The telephone is underneath the stairs;
the names go on and on, mostly in pairs.

III

I can see you on a beach in Spain
in a long red dotted gown
your sudden laugh a rollicking refrain.

Your spackled well-cropped mane—
your face not tan but brown—
I can see you on a beach in Spain

then, with a click, I see you again
swimming as if you could never drown
your sudden laugh a rollicking refrain.

Pictures fade but some remain
engrained like a lifelong frown;
I can see you on a beach in Spain:

the way you lean back on your hands is plain
though sometimes I strain to capture the sound
of that sudden laugh, that rollicking refrain.

There are too many pictures in Scottish rain
at a nondescript inn, a sepia town
but I see you on a beach in Spain—
your sudden laugh a rollicking refrain.

IV

The raven died alone, searching for land—
never mentioned again, once out of sight.
This death, unseen, is hard to understand.

(Your ship caught fire. The lifeboats were manned
by panicky sailors who left you behind in the night.)
The raven died alone, searching for land;

the pulse of her wings grew fainter as she scanned
the flood for a branch to bring back and finish her flight,
but her death, unseen, is hard to understand.

(With the lifeboats gone, we thought you might build a grand
kind of raft, like Kon-Tiki, and head for home, despite
the raven who died alone, searching for land.)

For years I imagined the raft as I planned
your arrival: warm blankets, a welcoming light—
because death, unseen, is hard to understand.

If only I'd witnessed its rigorous hand,
I'd be finished with sorrow, free of this passion to write
of the raven who died alone, searching for land—
of your death, not seen, too hard to understand.

V

I've never told you this before
but I can't imagine you dead—
a piece of flotsam drifting toward the shore.

Since you've been gone I've talked to you more
in spite of your silence, my lingering dread
but I've never told you this before:

when I try to picture you, your laugh is no more;
a featureless face floats softly away from your head—
a piece of flotsam drifting toward the shore.

The sailors who found you wrote me a letter I tore
into tiny confetti—enough had already been said.
I've never told you this before

but night after night in dreams I was cold to the core
as I struggled through icy water, burgundy red,
while pieces of flotsam drifted toward the shore.

I no longer dream one day you'll walk through the door
and your voice doesn't haunt me, late in bed.
I've never told you this before
but your words are like flotsam drifting toward the shore.

VI

When I stand on the shore, I wonder where you are
somewhere in that fathomed room behind
the waves like doors that slowly swing ajar.

Dappled stones at my feet are smeared with tar,
sucked by the undertow, they jostle and grind
while I stand on the shore, wondering where you are.

Beyond the raging surf, beyond the bar,
in your green chamber you hide, forever blind
to the waves like doors that slowly swing ajar

inviting me in, enticing me from afar,
but their curling crests are an unmistakable sign
I should stay on shore and wonder where you are.

Your voice in the wind doesn't say where you are
and I listen less and less, resigned
to those waves like doors that slowly swing ajar.

Will the light of the crescent moon, the northern star
create a pathway we both can find
as I stand on the shore wondering where you are
and the waves like doors slowly swing ajar?

PART TWO

Salobreña Notebook

Off Season

October's the month for storage.
—*Sylvia Plath*

Someone's burning something on the sand.
Smoke drifts; there is no wind,
just a band

of heat haze blurring the horizon
so the sea, white with sun,
travels on

into the white of the sky; out there
where boats sail in the air,
sea gulls jeer.

Each day one more beach cafe is closed;
today the *Flores* lost
its roof first

as they pulled down the wattle sunshade,
brittle and frayed; homemade
smells fading:

garlic and soup; *patatas fritas;*
fish with fried tomatoes;
tortillas—

all hauled off in a truck, leaving bare
concrete floors for winter,
nothing more.

Only two remain: *Los Faroles*,
back from this beach, which frills
for ten miles

the waving acres of sugar cane,
and *El Peñon*, leaning
its bleached beams,

like picked bones, against the pock-marked rock.
Here, flotsam is plastic
or old sacks;

two women swim through the clear water:
you can hear their laughter,
the clatter

of cups from the bar, and the lapping
waves that lightly slap the
old riprap.

Salobreña Storms

They gather darkly over the sea.
Prowling the horizon
they frown and glower,
woken before their time.
For a while they tromp the hills
behind the village
warning us of their presence
with the shimmer of baleful glances.

They stamp and pout like children
but the village ignores them
till someone nervously cracks a joke
and they swoop on us, agile.
Huge furry forearms arc overhead,
swipe the soft skin of the heavens
and rip it apart with their claws:
a dazzling mass bursts from sudden seams.

We are lost in their rage—
no longer capable of joke or argument.
We give up all pretence of normal life
and set aside the baking or today's paper.
On balconies, we inhale each electric spill,
but now that we are all eyes their fury abates;
they tire of faces at windows, move through
in search of less sycophantic souls.

We watch the fur of their behinds
as they stumble across the plain, muttering.
As the last huge foot flicks across the mountains
we burst out with our own shrill noise.
Now we are the naughty children,
exclaiming as our grim fathers leave the room.
Reaching for marzipan and muscatel wine,
we fancy ourselves survivors once again.

Fiesta Mayor, 1987

Day One

Rockets rush up from the *ayuntamiento*;
there's a long pause, sometimes a bang,
once in a while a colored star or two
but more often they fizzle and fall.
Fiesta lights span the narrow streets,
hooked up with tape, trailing live wires
so each time it rains, everything shorts.
On the empty lot, among rusty cans and cigarette butts
a boy plays guitar hour after hour,
his voice crying out the *cante hondo*
of this southern land. Families gather
in upstairs living rooms, tables laden with sponge cake
and *turrón*. Clothes wilt on the roof
as voices rise to drown the blaring TV.
Sweet wine in a *purrón* goes hand to hand while
downstairs, the mule's eyes are full of flies.

Day Two

Outside the town hall, the town band
blows and bangs its way through Sousa and de Falla,
the brass wavering like the sound track
on a home movie. Women watch from balconies
as the *paseo* below slows down. Two young men
in skin-tight jester pants giggle and point
till the crescendo ends in a clash of cymbals
and silence holds the crowd for a moment.

When the piccolo trills, heads turn and murmur again
and the two boys sidle close, thigh enticing
striped thigh in a sensuous caress. Around them
older men in grey workshirts smoke black tobacco
and remind me of those men, twenty years ago,
who told me of the soldier shot dead by *guardias*,
his body left to rot on the road to the camp.
He was a *maricón*, they said, and shrugged and spat.

Day Three

After the rainstorm, steam rises
from the streets and the dust stays down
but clouds hang over the sea—
a dark curtain behind the platform
on the beach. The priest raises his arms
as if he's just stepped out from heaven
flanked by grandiose pillars of cumulus:
all he needs is a bolt of lightning
and he will be declared an angel!
He blesses the crowd; guitarists take the stage.
Soon wild girls stamp and flounce,
their ruffles whirling crimson and teal blue.
Even the smallest child snaps her fingers
and looks down her Andalusian nose.
Her skirt, flashing yellow as a mustard field,
dazzles your eye in front of the black sky.

Searching for the Grave
Gibraltar, 1987

1

What I remember most is the heat.
Usually I find its touch benign
but there it seemed hostile—
particularly to those under the ground
which was baked to concrete.
I wondered what it had done to the bones below.

Bones should decompose gently
in leaf mould or sticky clay;
fall apart softly
like boiled chicken wings
amid busy beetles and worms
underground.

But there—who knows? Were they set hard,
caught solid, like those pieces of white almond
in the amber clarity of toffee?
Were all those dead people—yes, my two as well—
trapped down there in their bones,
denied their slow return to the sap?

What a place to get your bones stuck!
What a place to sit it out, dreaming of
turfy churchyards, stream banks, even
that chalky Sussex soil you knew so well,
inhospitable to your flowers, but home.

I remember walking in the heat on dusty paths
past peeling benches between slabs of stone.
We must have read thousands of names
then we went back and read them again.
I remember, too, how the man looked
when he said *yes, they could be*
under that patch of blackberries
(six feet tall and spreading fast).

> *Why would they haul in stones*
> *like these pebbles crunching under my feet?*
> *This is not Brighton beach but Spanish soil,*
> *perched on the cusp of Africa and Europe.*
> *British policemen play house on the rock;*
> *this is Gibraltar. Even the dead are imported.*

2

> *Listen, I've come a long way to find you*
> *stuck here in this white-hard ground.*
> *Distant machinery bothers the air*
> *but nothing moves, not even lizards*
> *crouched in the cracks between crumbling bricks*
> *and I seem to be stuck with the dead.*

What I remember most is
that one red hibiscus bloom
we picked beside the peeling bench
and laid on the broken headstone
when, at last, we found it—
the flower I could not place there myself

knowing it would wither in the fierce sun
knowing I would not bring another to take its place
knowing that your stone was broken
your bed baked hard and
the blackberries growing closer
week by week.

Right at the End of El Peñon

I am as much at sea as I can be
without a boat, bottle-green deeps below
on three sides. Sounds of gravel truck
and mule train float across the water, muffled
as if in a corked bottle from another world.
This place has its own quietness
embracing the rust-colored bird
that flits among twigs of silver thyme
sprung from chinks in the rock.

A man fishes from a yellow boat a long way out,
the creak of his oarlocks distinct.
Beside me, on a pink striated boulder,
sits the child I used to be, watching her father
a distant figure in a tweed hat
hunched in one rowboat or another.
Wrapped in my school raincoat, I peer through mist
as the rhythm of his reel sweeps across the loch.
From the oaks on the bank of Wisden Pond
I listen to the hissing line he casts.

A few sunbeams break the sky's weak spot
and fall in straight lines, pointing.
They are pointing down; their stiff fingers
pierce the surface, as if to pick out
the quick trout flashing through fresh water—
though here they light on tuna and sea bream
pink at the gills. More and more fingers
descend from dark clouds saying *look! look!*
but I already know how it looks from far away—
the fisherman's shaded face; the shape of patience.

The House on the Bluff

Sometimes it wishes it could tiptoe
down the hillside, pick its way
among rocks and olives and stonecrops,
dip its toes in the green sea,
instead of just sitting on this ledge
gazing, gazing over infinite water
while the sun seeps into its soft white walls.

Obligingly, it casts its shadow
over the musk of the grape arbor, but
sometimes at night it thinks of diving
straight down: imagine the emerald explosion
as phosphorescence bursts from its plunge
and droplets flash as they rocket away
like fireflies caught napping!

But in the morning, as the sun rises,
the house squats down ready to take the weight
again on its terra cotta tiles.
Red peppers beam as the first rays
reach their roof; geraniums nudge
each other awake on the terrace;
the bougainvillaea stretches and sighs.

The High Villages

To live in the Alpujarras
is to live on the rim of the sky,
that upturned bowl a blue mass
so close you can lift up your face
with a morning song
and breathe azure into your lungs.

Surely Atlas was born here
where almost anyone could hold up
the sky with one hand—
it they weren't using both hands
to knead the olive oil dough into loaves
and slide them into the wood-burning stove;

or to thresh grain through sieves,
sweeping and shaking the round frames
like giant tambourines;
or to pull down milk in streams—
left right, left right into buckets
from the scaly teats of a hundred goats.

In Capileira we ate rabbit with alioli.
Our window overlooked the flat rooftops
of Moorish houses: molded gullies,
peppers drying by ceramic chimney pots,
and the Poqueira Gorge below, a sudden surprise
between barely parted thighs.

As we clambered down there
two women with baskets went by, dressed in black,
stockings rolled down to old tennis shoes.
They planned to gather nuts until dark,
they said, but they passed many good walnut trees,
crossed the river, and climbed the opposite hillside

quilted with squares of vegetation.
Beside a slate hut, a woman worked
alone with a grey horse, the isolation
of her life hard for us to comprehend.
Perhaps the nut gatherers had a distant field
of their own? Perhaps there was a child

in the slate house— a child who left
before dawn to climb to the school
opposite her home, perched above the cleft.
Watching from close to the sky, I felt like a fool
for seeing in all this poverty something rich—
something as close as the sky I could almost touch.

La Bruja del Sueño*

She has one eye, slightly on the left
   of her face, which is an egg.
She looks at you balefully with this eye
   when you turn the corner
by the blue-white wall, where sunlight
   bleaches her patch of dust.

You know you should be afraid
   of her one-eyed stare
but you can't remember why. Does she know
   about the cold spring
that erupts in your belly—the outer limits
   like precipitous horizons

you cannot yet approach and
   sail across, proving
once and for all you are the explorer
   you claim to be?
So what if she sees all this? Still,
   you wonder, why be afraid?

It must be, you think, because one eye
   is considered insufficient
to see both past and future. But
   she looks at you carefully
as you round the angle of the wall
   and you know it is not so.

* The Witch in the Dream

36

She sees, with her one good eye,
    who the explorers are.
You fear the horizons—she will tell you so,
    and chuckle too, sometimes maliciously.
But you will sail towards the edge, she says,
    when the tides are right.

PART THREE

The Dyke With No Name

The word *lesbian* must be affirmed
because to discard it is to collaborate
with silence and lying about our
very existence; with the closet-game,
the creation of the *unspeakable*.

— Adrienne Rich

The Hero

Five o'clock; winter street; soggy leaves
like tea leaves left in the pot.
Tea time and dark as the dyke with no name
passes lighted windows to other lives—
fires burning inside.

She is twelve; alone. There will be crumpets
for tea. Till then she is the hero:
she plunges her hand into the wolf's foaming mouth,
grasps the muscle of its tongue
and twists until it drops;

Molly is tied to the tree in need of rescue—
unless, of course, she's drowning in heavy swell.
Sometimes she grabs in panic at the hero, who
gently but firmly knocks her out cold on the chin,
tows the limp body to shore.

Five o'clock; alone. Her footsteps echo
yet Molly is beside her asking questions.
The dyke with no name is telling all her secrets,
eyes alive as they walk by lighted windows—
fires burning inside.

Dirty Panes

Down by the greenhouse
her friends were discussing boys.
The dull pop of a ball
from the courts beyond
kissed the air
like the plump burps of the frogs
that bobbed up and down
through the slime on the lily pond.

Down by the greenhouse Lottie was telling all:
his hands and where they went,
his scratchy face.
The one on the edge of the group
examined the wall—
the curve of each rounded pebble
each folded crevice.

Inside the greenhouse,
strictly out of bounds,
Lottie was telling them
all about french kissing:
the tongue…the lips…like this…
she grabbed at Rose
and kissed her full on the mouth,
bodies pressing.

Condensation ran down
the dirty panes
as the dyke with no name
sucked in the steamy air.
She tried to laugh like her friends
but her mouth was locked
to hold in the words of her heart
that rose like a prayer.

Sex Knocks at the Door

and she is supposed to do it, to want it

but she wants to ride her horse alone
on the swathe of downland; wants to breathe in

the exhaled green breath of grasses
and the long blue sigh of the sky.

She inhales the smoke and cappuccino steam
of the coffee bar, crosses one nylon knee

over the other, meets people at appointed times
noted in her leather diary and sometimes

if they kiss her, she notes that too
with a secret symbol.

At last her breasts grow and she has a boyfriend
who plays the trumpet and smells of fried things.

When he kisses her in the thatched pavilion
by the tennis courts, she thinks his tongue

feels like a slug but then she has another
boyfriend who has golden skin. She has done "well."

This one stays over in the spare room
and her parents are behind closed doors.

She sleeps with her head on his chest
proud of herself because her girlfriends approve.

She doesn't touch him below the line of blond
hairs that creeps down from his navel,

they never do it because she doesn't want to,
and somehow he is not a real person.

Sex Knocks at the Door—2

When the woman (who is very real)
asks about her soul she tells
everything.

The woman is twenty years older
sends her poems she does not
understand;

perhaps you are my long lost daughter
she says, or: *we are such soulmates
are we not?*

Darling, she says; her voice rattles the
larynx. She plays Piaf over
and over.

Once beside the river their eyes lock.
The woman holds her whole body
in her gaze

and she wants to look away but the
water swirls by and she shudders
down inside

and throbs somewhere she has never throbbed
before. Something real and large is
happening

and sex, not the idea but the
animal itself, is knocking
at the door.

Acts of Love

She turns the key smoothly
lock slips across like a caress
door sweeps open for the older woman's
smooth glide into the low seat
knees lifted and twisted in
smile right into the eyes.

She feels the older woman observe
the blue veins on the backs of her
tanned hands—these hands
holding and turning the fast car
through narrow lanes—hands precise
and strong. Hero's hands.

She never wanted to be a man, just a hero;
she knew how to love heroines, but not
how to be one. No one taught her
to walk on the outside or give up her coat
in the rain; she knew all along.
But she never wanted to be a man.

Every year on her birthday she hopes
someone will send flowers: long-stemmed
red roses delivered to her door,
extravagant bundles of fragrance.
Year after year, even now, she imagines
the card in its tiny envelope.

No Name

Do you ever touch yourself there?
the older woman asks
when they are naked.
Do it when I'm not there
and think about me.

But when she thinks about the older woman
fear curls through her whole body
and fear and sex together
chill her skin
till she does not know which is which.

I can't help myself
though I know it's wrong
she writes to the older woman
between parties and dates and
staying up late with a bottle of cheap wine.

The older woman looks for beautiful young men
and often says *when you get married…*
When I get married, repeats the dyke with no name,
when I get married, when I get married,
when I get married…

but all she knows are the perfect lines
of the older woman's fingers
which know her body
and the small crisp tongue which darts
among her teeth

and the throbbing which never stops
and the fear which is sex and the sex
always knocking at the door, the sex
which means she can't help herself, the sex
which is also fear and which has no name.

Cryptic

Questions require answers
require stories
require lies.

A believable life;
account of time
spent. Something

to discuss with a best
friend who must not
know. Loving

means denying: smother
the fire in the
truthful eyes.

Loving means censor the
pronouns, rehearse
fictions for

best friend, for family.
It is said they
cannot know.

It is said they must not
know. *Somebody
called:* do not

ask "was it a woman?"
Somebody called:
smother the

fire. *Hey, somebody called:*
if you are a
friend, don't look

in the eyes—you must not
know; oh no, you
must not know.

Sleepwalking

The older woman was gone
though they never broke up;
how could you end a thing
if you couldn't mention it?

    Was she awake or asleep
    when she said to some lover:
    "Let's run away to an island—
    just you and me"? Was it a dream
    they'd be safe across the sea?

"Write me your thoughts,"
the psychiatrist looked at the clock.
"Useless" she wrote in her diary
and never went back.

    But the older woman's voice
    never left her alone:
    when you get married (that voice
    she had always known). *When I get
    married*, she thought, *when I get married….*

Organ and bells were triumphant
the day the dyke with no name
got married. She wore a white gown
and two hundred people came.

    Did she go through it asleep
    or wide awake? The older woman
    was drunk— she nodded and nodded.
    "So now you are married," she said,
    "yes, now you are married."

The Wedding Album

Plump covers of white leather restrain pages
like strangers in suede gloves, introduced,
fingertips barely touching.

Pages threaded with a cord of silk pull tight
but well worn creases at the margin
ensure they turn and will turn

through generations, though the silken knot merge
fiber by fiber into itself,
unpickable.

*

She turns the first page headed "Guests",
the blue ink of names fading. Who
were they

these strangers in morning coats, hats,
June dresses, sipping champagne? She
turns again:

the program, printed in silver,
proclaims her escorted to *The
Water Music*,

serenaded by hymn and psalm
("Praise My Soul", "To Be a Pilgrim",
"The King Shall Rejoice"),

then one half of "man and wife", ringed,
blessed, and processed in the vestry
to a Bach toccata.

She turns the page before fanfare
and march (the woman crying in
the third pew was her lover).

In the photo, her hair and smile
hold stiff in wind, lace hides goose flesh
but not the questions in her eyes.

*

Now she picks at the silk knot with
bitten nails, pulls one strand loose with
her teeth, and then another,

draws the cord slowly through pages'
holes till it slips free and all the
leaves reluctantly shake loose

like long hair untied, clinging for
a moment to the shape of the
day. With scissors and colored

paper she fashions a new page,
punches holes, carefully rethreads
the string. On this purple page

she pastes another photo: the
camera looks up at her head
against a white ceiling.

She is talking; a frown between
her eyes, hands on her hips; hair flies
from her head, tangled curls.

And now, loud and clear, she speaks out.
Now, her voice echoes through the room.
Now—now she proclaims her name.

PART FOUR

A Memoir

Fish

I AM STANDING at the draining board in our rented apartment looking down at a neat row of fish. I don't know what they are, since the fish market in this small Andalusian village is too noisy for me to hear the names, which probably don't correspond, anyway, to the correct Castilian they taught me at school.

The fish are whole. Each one has a head, a tail and a body, all joined together. And inside, guts. Each head has two eyes, which stare as I wave the small, sharp knife around in the air and contemplate the removal of these guts—a job I have never had to do before, although I am forty-three years old. Something about this gives me pause. I am hearing my mother's voice. Memories of my father hover around too, although I never hear his voice; he visits me in a series of blurred images, always at a distance, and often with a fishing rod in his hand. There was one summer, I remember, when I tried to bridge that distance, a summer when my mother's voice temporarily faded out and my father's image grew sharper....

* * *

That summer—1954 I think it was—I tried fishing. Really tried. Before that, I had often gone with my father to row the boat, and I knew how to dip the oars without splashing as we stalked the big trout off the island at Posingworth Lake. I knew, too, how it felt hunched in the bow of the motorboat two miles off Shoreham, as we trolled for mackerel, and how slowly time passed when we sat with our lines out, bottom fishing, while the swell rolled under us with a corkscrew twist that left my stomach hanging. But I wasn't really committed.

My mother despised fishing. She refused to have anything to do with it, although sometimes she would come out to Posingworth late in the day with a picnic tea, and we'd all sprawl on damp needles, where pines stood guard in front of the rhododendron wall. Once, choosing a patch of sun-warmed bracken, I almost sat on two adders coiled like an anchor rope still gleaming from the water.

Even though I admired my mother's tirades against those fools who hung around all day waiting for fish to swallow their hooks, from time to time I would go off with the men—my father and brother, my brother-in-law (under duress), and occasionally our family doctor, a Scot with a deadly accurate cast. My mother had long since given up: she got sick when it was sea fishing, and sometimes even on a mirror-smooth lake; she hated the smell of wet wool; and it was, she said, *quite dreadful* when you caught one. The final insult was that she had to clean the fish my father caught, so we could cook them on the campfire and eat them with blackened potatoes in tin foil.

"We're not all that poor," she used to say. "The fishmonger has nice fresh trout and they come with the innards already out"—my mother would never say *guts*—"and no heads either. I can't stand the way they look at you with those reproachful pop-eyes."

It was my mother who pointed out every year that the trout season opened on April 1st, and what more fitting comment could there be than that. And it was she who turned every mishap into a family story, poking fun at the fishermen. For example, when the three men went out from Brighton beach one freezing Boxing Day and capsized in the surf on their way in again, my mother recounted the event with triumphant satisfaction to all her bridge friends. Could my father really have dived down over and over as she described, surfacing only to yell: "The fish, the fish! Save the fish!" while my brother tried to prevent the boat from being swept out to France, and my brother-in-law staggered around the beach in confusion because he had lost his glasses? I do remember that night, in the dress circle of the Theatre Royal, my father and brother sneezing through the play, while my brother-in-law, who couldn't see where the stage was, snored loudly. My mother's expression conveyed her certainty that this was the final proof: fishing was either caused by, or led to, insanity.

More often than not in these early years, I threw my lot in with my mother and sister, who spent a good deal of time playing the piano, the viola, and the record player. I joined them with my array of recorders and, later, my clarinet. Until the summer of '54, that is, when, at the age of ten, I temporarily abandoned the female stronghold and joined the hard core anglers, which had the overtones of a significant choice in a family that was divided along gender lines into two camps: the sportsmen on one side, the musicians and artists on the other.

As usual, my father organized our holiday around fishing and we went to Scotland, just the three of us, since my brother and sister were old enough to holiday by themselves. The hotel in the highlands was a huge stone mansion, once the seat of some powerful clan with its own tartan, whose crest still adorned the plates and silverware. Seen from the long approach across a heather-covered moor, it made sense of that Scots word *dour:* it cried out for mist and howling dogs—but in vain. That summer the sun shone and the sky was blue, and I was enchanted.

We stayed at Craiglynne for three weeks and the first week was warm, though a cool breeze ruffled the surface of the belfry pool, where "the old preacher," a salmon reputed to weigh at least thirty-five pounds, was believed to live. Inside the hotel's two-foot thick, stone walls, it was cool and dark, and in the library there was always a blazing wood fire, which someone told us they lit every day, year in year out. For two or three days, I retreated to one of the chimney seats and read my way through numerous Agatha Christies and James Bonds. After lunch, my mother would insist that I join her in a brisk walk on the moors with the dogs.

As the weather got hotter and stiller in the second week, I took to wandering on the moors by myself. One day, I sat on a rock high above the river, which cut a path through purple heather and was flanked by bands of lush grass rapidly fading to brown. Two lines of silver birches sprouted from this grass, shading the banks. Down there below the bend, where the current swept wide into a pool, my father stood in his thigh-waders, casting upstream. I watched him for a long time as he moved slowly towards the pool, throwing the line rhythmically, his head shaded by a tweed hat which, I knew, was stuck full of flies, though I couldn't see them from my viewpoint. I watched him untangle his line from one of the birches, patiently clinging to a root with one hand while he worked the fly free with the other. If he muttered, I was too far away to hear; up there on the wide moor, I could hear only the cries of buzzards and the occasional chirp of a grasshopper. I watched for a very long time and then decided that this summer I would catch my first salmon.

My father was surprised by my sudden enthusiasm. I demanded use of the small rod, a supply of flies in a tackle box, and my own permit. Waders didn't matter: I simply put on my very small pink shorts and some old tennis shoes which would allow me to clamber over the rocky river bottom. This was unorthodox and made my father uncomfortable, but he acquiesced, only too glad of some support in the family. Indeed his jubilation was such that I later wondered if he battled a few pangs of guilt at dragging my mother and me along on these fishing trips.

We strode off together in the early morning, laden with canvas bag and fish basket, landing net and tackle box. At the river we would separate, each to our own beat, which saved me the embarrassment of admitting how many flies I lost in the birch trees. I really wanted to catch a salmon. Surely, if I cast the fly just right and hit those deep pools under the tree roots, I'd feel the fish grab. But nothing happened. Morning after morning, in between the hours I spent hooking tussocks of grass, clusters of leaves, and sometimes even my own clothes, I made several perfect casts. But not one of them enticed a salmon.

I was easily disheartened. It didn't seem fair that perfect casting did not result in fish. I could understand not catching one when the line was wound around a tree trunk, or the fly slapping the water with a huge leaf attached to it, but I couldn't accept that perfect skill should go unrewarded. It never had before: if I studied, I passed the exams—in fact, I often passed without studying; if I practised the piano, I could play Bach preludes from memory. But here was something I wanted badly and was prepared to learn to do right, and it wasn't working. I couldn't make that large silver fish swirl to the surface and grab my fly.

My father said the river was too low. The hotel proprietor said it was the heat. The gillie said it was the laird over the hill, who had diverted too much water from his stream to irrigate a rock garden. The only consolation was that nobody else caught anything either. The stuffed fish in glass cases on each landing of the wide staircase seemed to be grinning with delight at all the disgruntled conversations. "Terrible weather," the guests agreed as they passed each other on the stairs in their plus fours or mid-calf tweed skirts, which never varied, despite the eighty-degree weather.

The third week was unprecedented as the thermometer crept towards ninety and the library fire went unlit. I stopped fishing altogether and found a spot where I could lie on the bank under the birch trees and look into one of the still pools. The water was clean and the pebbles on the bottom distinct. Their bluish grey tones reminded me of the beach and seemed incongruous here in this clear brown water, flowing between peat banks. The sun pierced the shade like a small spotlight and gnawed into the small of my back till sweat began to run down towards my waist.

I had been lying like this for an hour or two one day, when I noticed what looked like some logs lying there, but it seemed unlikely as the branches of the overhanging trees were much more slender than these hefty objects. Suddenly, one of the logs turned around—not fast, but not pushed by the current either. It turned quite deliberately and faced the other way. Immediately, I saw that the logs were salmon, six of them, basking in the tropical water.

"Only way anyone could catch salmon in that state of mind would be by dapping," grunted my father, when I told him what I had seen. "The river's probably full of the lazy beasts just lying there. You can see them easily in this weather."

For the rest of our vacation, I wandered the river banks spotting salmon. Anywhere the current was not too fast, you could see them, fat and happy. A few fish fell to an illegally dapped fly upstream from the hotel, and the dining room buzzed with the news when the poacher was caught, but mostly they just lay around as if they, too, were on holiday, and I grew very fond of them. My mother and I and the dogs walked as usual and the men, cooped up in the hotel with nothing to do but boast of other years when the weather was better, fumed. And every day I went to look at the happy salmon, until I knew without a doubt that my mother was right: it would be *quite dreadful* if I caught one.

That was almost my last attempt at fishing and at infiltrating my father's world. My mother never said a word about it, though I'm sure she was glad to have me back. She enjoyed that holiday and always spoke of it with a certain fondness. I'm not sure if it was because the men were frustrated in their foolishness, or if it was because of my obvious pleasure at the salmon's refusal to cooperate….

* * *

I am standing over the pink-gilled Spanish fish with a knife in my hand and my mother's voice is complaining: "I do wish they'd sell them with the innards *out*." In my mind, the fishmonger becomes my father, imposing this messy task on us females. And my father…where is he? Has he, as usual, deposited his fish and disappeared until they are cleaned, cooked, and sitting on a plate? Why is he so damned invisible?

As I make a neat incision into the belly of the first fish, I remember that the summer at Craiglynne was not, in fact, my last attempt to make sense of my father's world. It must have been '66 or thereabouts, after both he and my mother were dead, when I found myself in Scotland again, touring for a few days with a friend. We stopped at a mill with a little shop. To my surprise, I purchased a tweed hat in soft heather tones. The next day I bought a fly rod and several boxes of flies, some of which I stuck into the hat. Then, armed with a permit and some boots, I strode over the moor to a small hill loch, where I fished in the mist for nine hours without seeing a single trout. My friend thought I was insane, and I hardly knew how to explain, driven by some urge I didn't understand myself. But that truly was my last attempt. To this day, the pleasures of fishing elude me, and my father has not yet emerged from the mist.

Still, slicing the undersides of these fish, scraping off the translucent scales, and piling the reproachful heads into the garbage, I am astonished at how familiar it all seems. I know how my mother would have felt about it as the scales glisten on my hands and the knife cuts clean. But I am quite enjoying the task. Somewhere along the way I must have learned there were more than two camps.

PART FIVE

History and Geography

Countries

Changing countries mid-life
is a bit like changing trains mid-town.
You step off the Bakerloo train—

that muddy brown path on the map—
where suspicious eyes peer over newspapers
(why are you leaving? where are you going?)

and board the District and Circle
whose green and yellow lines
drag memories of springtime across each tube plan

above each vicious sliding door.
"STAND CLEAR OF THE DOORS"
and they hiss with gusto

as you stumble towards a new life
hoping they will not squeeze you
in their impersonal grip

and the whole train watch
as you cry out, stuck
with one foot in each world.

*

To change countries mid-life
is to change mealtimes, tax forms,
the shape of mailboxes

and to discover that green and white
chalk hills falling down to the grey sea
are etched into your heart.

Dutiful at first, you admire forests of Douglas fir
but they roll away on such a grand scale
that you long for an unassuming pigsty

or a shearing shed between
narrow pathways of mud.
You miss leaning on gates

to discuss the weather with strangers
and footpaths from which you glimpse
the private lives of back gardens.

You miss a particular smell of salt and chalk
carried by massive winds from the Channel
and the almost-white cliffs

turning blunt faces towards France,
their toupees of bright green turf
threatening to lift and sail away.

*

You know how to love those soft valleys
(in spite of the miseries you know they hide)
where you simply happened to be born.

There, your heart knows the difference
between a politician and an oak tree.
But here, when your heart begins to stir

in the arroyos and mesas of O'Keeffe,
(giant mouth of petal hinting at stamen;
sandstone canyon and dwelling;

words carved out of rock; sage in the nose
and insects rolling their R's),
you wonder, can you trust your heart's response?

Should you adopt this new landscape,
this powerful sky? And is to choose
a land also to choose a people?

Out to Grass

Day after day I stroll the orchard,
hang my head over the gate
as they leave the pub singing. Sometimes

they bring a cox's orange pippin or
juicy russet if I time it right
and there's always the burgundy clover

sweet as the treats from Sunday crowds.
After the church bell peals
I watch them all in their hats

the swarm of cars buzzing up
the lane and ploughman's lunches
served at white iron tables with scrolls

like the mangers at the blacksmith's place
in Hurstpierpoint—the one who used fire
on my feet and clicked his teeth.

I'd snort and show the whites of my eyes
as the smoke rose like November bonfires
but he just shrugged and clicked his teeth

some more so I stopped. Now when ice
films my trough and crusty ruts bruise
my unshod hoofs, she brings hot bran mash

and strokes my neck, speaking to me
of the children who are long gone.
They grew too big for trophies and rosettes

for caning me over the painted poles
and crying into my braided mane
after victory or defeat. She rubs warm grease

into my stiff fetlock and tells me
I am old. It's true I can no longer see
the ridge of the downs above the Norman tower

but I remember how it is up there
when the spring wind blows salt up your nose
and the grasses bow and scrape

as you part them with your flashing feet
and your bright new shoes
cut crisp arcs into the ancient chalk.

How Words Can Drive You Crazy

1

At the end of our orchard
when I was five
the plums had a purple sheen;
if you stroked them one way
then the other, the color changed
like a thick pile carpet.

"Victorias" my mother said;
"run and pick me the ripest
victorias." She was regal
flour on her hands
apron tied no nonsense
her voice imperious.

2

My sister and I spelled out
word after word at dinner:
"*About*, silly, not *a boat*"
she sighed, and I willed
about into my brain
every day through slow summer

till one day the word
repeated over and over
grew absurd
sound with no sense
all words merging
and the black hole blinked.

3

Then there were books
with words I said to myself
all wrong, till they became mine.
"*O*-rang *to*-rang" I sang
the monkey in the book
as bright as sherbet

brilliant orange acrobat
in her leafy jungle
till years later
someone said "*orang*utan"
and for an instant
the black hole blinked again.

4

When the King died
I learned to sing
"God Save the Queen"
before curtain up or
after the film. I sang
"her" instead of "him":

"Send her victorious
happy and glorious"—
year after year *victorias*
till the black hole loomed again:
the song was not about my mother
the song was not about plums!

Mother and Daughter at the Y

They're always there together,
the younger one about my age.
I pretend not to look sideways
in front of the long mirror
where we blow dry.

Eastern European genes, I guess
and their four brown eyes
dance around as they pat
and poke at each other's thick hair.
They look alike, even under water—
identical black swimsuits against
the blue tile at the shallow end.

Last week when I came down lap 32
I could see through misted goggles
their four feet moving slow motion
and I knew they were talking as usual—
hands completing words in fast motion
through the light chemical air.

At the turn, my head bobbed out
and I carried a snatch of laughter
away up the straight, thinking
what would it be like
to have a mother as a friend?

Towards the end of 34 I looked left:
they were still there. This time

one pair of legs—the younger pair—
was planted, feet apart
in the stance of peasant legs
that know their ground and work it.

The mother floated, arms limp,
elbows sinking in abandon,
her daughter's hand firm
under the small of her back.
I bobbed and turned:
what would it be like?

Laps 36 and 38 I look straight ahead
at the approaching wall feeling
my spine stretch thin, my chest open.
Breathe, pull, kick I think
until thought merges with water
and I see again the back view
of that woman I once followed breathless
through a crowd until she turned
and I remembered: my mother is dead.

Breathe, pull, kick I no longer think
as I carry her absence up the lane
waterlogged, yet slicing still
through the pool's soft mass.
At 40, the daughter's by the wall.
The mother swims a few fast strokes,
arms sprawling, head high out of the water.
The daughter laughs and reaches out her hands.

Still Life

A piece of coral, white and small
sits on my table, curved around
a bluish marble someone found
in an antique desk, in the pigeon hole.
Nobody knows who put it there
or how the coral came to lie
so perfectly, just like an eye
around its pupil's glassy stare.
Together these two objects seem
to glare at me as if I knew
where each belonged, where each should go.
If only I knew, I'd split them up
and make them become themselves again,
for this is my dead father's gaze, I know.

Another Quarrel

It had none of the wild abandon
of flamenco dancers
their heads tossed in disdain
bodies flung away
in a shrug spiralling head to heel
petulant feet
punishing the boards, all fingers firing.

It did not fall in a crazy curve
like the trapeze artist
swooping from her canvas vault
riding gravity
to the summit, heart-stopping pause
then falling again
to sweep out the hollow air with her razzle dazzle.

Instead, we wore the sedate kilt.
Our sporrans bobbed
as our feet, pointed and neat,
stepped deftly over
crossed swords, their edges gleaming
like shards of ice
while the bagpipes keened and keened.

The Bee Sting

Your feet in red wool socks stick
straight up, protrude from the grey
blanket, like those dead
feet that slide from their holes
in mortuary walls on TV.
It is mid-summer, but you shiver

with cold and adrenalin, while I shiver
with fear, afraid this film might stick
like they sometimes do on public TV
leave us frozen here with your grey
face immobile, two needle holes
in your thigh, not really dead

but somehow conjuring you dead
and me on this low stool, sitting shiva
while heat burns slow holes
through the film, which will not unstick
and move on, lift the grey
from your face, offer a miracle as on TV.

Beyond the curtain, nurses drink tea, ve-
hemently debate the reason someone's dead.
Your iron bed on wheels is peeling grey;
it's hot in here where even curtains shiver.
Thickets of tubes climb around and stick
into odd machines connected to holes

in the ceiling; labels on pigeonholes
beside me read: s*calpels, gloves, remote-TV,
blood sets:* ticker tape names that stick
on *(probably how they label dead
bodies at the morgue)*. I shiver,
check time, wait for you to open your grey-

green eyes. There's a glimpse of grey
sky through the skylight, shifting holes
in the clouds promising blue. You shiver
awake, roll your head weakly like a TV
star. Right on time you meet the dead-
line; things begin to seem less drastic.

"So why do *you* look grey?" you ask. I shiver:
your eyes are still holes, but you don't look dead.
The TV flickers as the film begins to unstick.

History and Geography

for Ruth

1

Your finger skims the map
dense with villages, towns, cities
of Russia and Eastern Europe.
You lean towards the blond
head of your brother-in-law
as you search through Bessarabia
and your father hunches over
the littered dinner table
passing on pieces of your mother's history—
your mother, who was the family historian.
You all ask questions
to which, mostly, there are answers
or at least speculations.
Not like my relatives, I think,
who say "what's the use?"
and "the past is the past."

2

You have your father's zany laugh.
It comes down to you from before
the events which flung him
from camp to flight to new world,
his family decimated.
That laugh rings back through
Germany and Austria, pogroms and seders,
tracking the history that is your home
as no country can ever be.

Is this why my relatives discard
their history—rooted in land so long
they have no need of a people?
My parents, living abroad
much of their lives
were sometimes called "expatriate"—
"away from the father land"—
but still and always
children of that father.
For you, changing countries without choice
is part of your history.
Surely there is no such thing
as an expatriate Jew
except, perhaps, a Jew outside history—
a Jew with no questions
wanting no answers.

3

The discarded map lies beside
pies and kugel, as the questions
and answers go on.
Leftovers become history.
This table becomes geography;
this room a small square, not marked
on the map, where countries each have
their own color: where countries
each have their own.

But what of this history,
this personal geography—
a patchwork of dining tables,
old documents, names culled from
telephone directories in strange cities?
Whose stories are missing
even from this family history,
where one unmarried aunt in Chicago
hides behind a post office box?
Has she chosen a life that does not fit
and written herself out
because she fears it will happen anyway?
Who will become the new expatriates
banished from the ranks of the banished?
Will your name be there, at some future table,
when they ask, "who were they—
those who went before?"
And will mine?
We choose not to write ourselves out
but to record our presence here tonight—
my blond head leaning toward yours,
our curious intersection
on a map that is larger, even
than the one your people trace
with such stubborn, loving care.

Fortieth Birthday Song

for Ruth

Crossing and joining
    and joining and crossing
and crossing and joining
    and joining and crossing.

There's gaining and losing
    there's childhood and older;
there's learning to let go
    and how to be bolder.
The past and the future—
    a chasm between;
the place we will go to
    and where we have been.

Sometimes it's hard to
    decide if this chasm's
the end of beginning
    or beginning the end.
One says you're losing
    the promise of childhood
The other's a trail—
    you can't see round the bend.

There's crossing alone
    though your friends are beside you,
there's picking your path
    and there's falling through space.

Though sometimes you want to
    turn back or to hide, you
are crossing each day
    to another new place.

The past and the future
    are coming together.
The past and the future
    are one and the same.
They meet and are joined
    whenever, wherever
you know who you are
    and you sing out your name.

Crossing and joining
    and joining and crossing
and crossing and joining
    and joining and crossing.

For a Friend whose Lover has Left

They say memory resides in the head
but I say it lives in the tips of fingers
the insides of thighs and forearms:
yes, the concave belly remembers
what it once embraced sleeping.

Your limbs remember skin; in sleep you reach
for someone whose name you have almost forgotten.
It is not your brain that recalls
the hollow above her collarbone
and the shoulder blade like a wing.

They say the brain's cells die with age.
You will forget the number you dialed
over and over, but one day your finger
will remember (as mine once did) leaping deftly
from the six to the four to the one.

You will not pay attention to the voice
that says "hello" because memories lurk
among whorls and scrolls of fingerprints.
"Sorry" you'll say and hang up, but still
your palm will hold the exact curve of her cheek.

Therapy

Your four walls were my frame
as I wove the tangled skein
and the hour hand traced its wedge-shaped boundary
around our sixty-minute once-a-week world.

I lived there as on a desert island
plucking the berries of childhood
gingerly tasting unfamiliar fruits—
always suspecting poison.

Desert island devotions—
unique in the dangerous frameless world
where stars glow beyond walls
and time spins the clock's face.

You changed color like a chameleon
and blended into my design.
The patterns emerged so clear and simple
they could break a heart.

Underworld

When the sun is low, low
locust trees with crisp spring pods
glow bright brown and amber.
I feel the photographer's urge
to catch their trunks while
twisted ropes of bark stand out
in the gleam of this angled footlight
like veins on some man's angry temple.

Strangely the slant light gives
ordinary trees a new stature.
They loom against wedgwood sky
menacing brittle blue with blazing arms.
Even the faded red barn looms—
its ordinary doorway a gaping mouth.

When the sun is lower still
all kinds of undersides reveal themselves:
gutters, eaves, partly burned beams—
a sudden illumination of the low
bringing unwonted light to the underexposed
as the spotlight slides away,
thrusting relentless rays
into an underworld that beats and brays.

Letters from Eastern Oregon
Hermiston: April, 1986

1

Magpies like cavorting clerics
stall midair with a flash of white surplice
and dive toward the brown Umatilla River
beyond my temporary terrace.

Each morning I stroll outside into air
heavy with blossom and cow dung.
The pair of yellow-bellied marmots in the field
skitters and scurries, tipsy with spring

while rams and long-eared goats butt heads
in slow-motion rites of the season;
like judo opponents, they bow carefully
and make it a solemn occasion.

2

I try not to think of what lies upwind
buried in tunnels of concrete,
beyond the huge sprinklers like minute hands
telling time for the thirsty winter wheat.

There's a pretty good chance that God will protect us
his house is on every block in town.
From the Latter Day Saints to the Lutheran school,
there's hardly a spot of unhallowed ground

as I drive to work past the First Baptist Church
and turn by the seat of the Nazarene.
The Wesleyans and the Catholics too—
by the end of the week, I swear I've seen

more churches than people, but nevertheless
my anxiety's not in the least assuaged.
Those bunkers hold five thousand tons of death—
I doubt even God is sufficiently enraged.

3

"Here comes the poet!" the children scream
their joy like a lover's kiss,
while six miles west, marsh hawks circle
above the organic phosphate nerve gas.

Up near the Catholic Church of our Lady
I stand in a classroom, reading aloud
the poems of nine-year-olds: one of them writes
of the night when her brand new stepdad vowed

to beat her till dawn for her sloppy ways.
Joshua, covered in green felt pen,
writes verses whose words sing songs on the page
and draws pictures of men in the klan.

"I like, I like, I like, I like,"
Xavier writes in tiny neat rows.
It's two days before I understand
that this is the only English he knows.

4

The wind in April rips up the air
you can hear it tear into strips
then moan and moan for what might have been
while sea gulls drift in like Viking ships.

It howls across the enormous plain
comes whistling through the gorge
snatches the spray from the upstart waves
that slap the bow of the plodding barge

then curtseys past the Golden Corral
flinging dust at the Desert Inn.
DeGroff's Mobile Village shudders and sways
as if in the grip of collective sin.

This town is far from the Catalan plain
where the *tramontana* rules;
the wind and I both travel abroad
uprooted like headstrong fools.

5

Each year the army invites the children
to visit its antelope, partridge and ducks.
Nothing is said of the rabbits who live
in the bunkers in cages, testing for leaks

and two years ago, four children broke in—
not on a tour but a plot of their own.
Later, three of them were injured by the bomb
they made with the booty they smuggled home.

Lucky they only ripped off dynamite—
no one out here is afraid of chemicals:
everyone knows they bring jobs to the town
(except for a few outsiders and radicals).

"If it weren't safe," the residents say,
"everyone here would certainly know."
So why do I worry, when falcons and quail
and golden eagles wheel above the depot?

6

Business is brisk at the Buggy Splash
as I head home from work past the Poodle Palace.
The pastures are green, the desert defeated
by hundreds of ditches: a westerner's Venice.

I drive home behind a red Chevy truck
past grazing mules whose glance is tranquil.
"God made men" reads the bumper sticker
"but Winchester made them equal."

The magpies are still doing aerial stunts
like black and white preachers on one final fling
while the marmots sit upright and sniff the wind.
Is something in the air this spring?

Prayer

In my 44th year I observe a cedar,
its staunchness of bark, its grace of bough,
and I want to pray, but don't know how
or to whom or what this tree has to do with

Mrs. Jackson, whose scripture lessons
required a basic blackboard sketch
week after week of the Holy Land—
coastline straight down, not much

ornament, just one jag and the Dead Sea
a third of the way up,
sometimes round as the full moon
sometimes egg-like, depending on her mood.

She drew it unbelievably fast
while we watched her back view in year-round
tweed skirt and lisle stockings,
planted like Gertrude Stein on the ground.

When she turned, we saw the odd plain on one side
of her chest, and some girls would stare.
(No one told us that Amazon warriors were
one-breasted women: *their* coastline was unfamiliar.)

We never thought of prayer as we plotted
Mrs. Jackson's progress through the days,
glimpsing through half-open doors
her chalk map with its bumpy nose—

silhouette of a land no one described
as disputed territory. She never explained
about the Jews now in Israel; they belonged
in the Bible, and there they remained

in their long robes and sandals,
begetting each other. They stayed in
their ancient world and we never wondered
what they had to do with praying

yet now I am quieted by the dignity
of this cedar, silenced by a star,
groping to understand the significance
of an emotion I think of as prayer.

Mrs. Jackson is dead. Too late to wonder
what she prayed for, or if she ever went to that
shell-shocked land, or why she stayed in school,
mapping holiness on every blackboard

but inspiring no reverence for geography,
no knowledge of unholy wars
and only now, years later,
this useless respect for her own battle scars.

Solo

Meadows fade toward the snowline;
rocks grow ambiguous in slant light;

five minutes ago they lay down
or stood dignified, minding their own business

but now they crouch and loom,
this one's face wrinkled: a bloodhound,

that one huge and stooped: Sasquatch
slipping into the shadow of the glacier.

I climb too fast
(can my heart stand it?)

dump the pack by a boulder
topped with bulging hippo eyes;

it peers over the pack as if
rising from a water hole.

I would laugh, but it's too quiet.
(Is this really laughter that chokes my lungs?)

Darker now, I make fire.
Hidden eyes lurk behind the footlights.

(What if I died here
dried sweat under my breasts

no life flight swooping over
the shoulder of the mountain?)

I know this scene. In a minute
the heart will calm its wild beating....

See! Here's the moon crawling
over the wedge of ice.

Come, shooting stars—
let the show begin.

Wilderness, High Tech

Orange and blue   life-saving
yellow   green like artificial
turf too bright   for tents and
packs   glaring at the true
colors of   moss and skunk
cabbage   bark and rose petal
Slippery nylon cords   D rings
water bottles   rubber straps
plastic paraphernalia   toys
The latest   aluminum tent
poles do not chime   like the
pipes of   the cathedral organ
but clink dead and   dull
unresponsive as a paper   plate

You lie on your back   in the
domed tent   staring at the
roof as if it were   the lofty
vault of   St. Paul's or
Canterbury   There's a cheap
fervent   thrill (though this is
no oversized shrine   full of
awe and fear)   The gaudy fabric
is lightweight   It repels rain
and fire   *(but not earth* you say
but not air)   You can carry
it for days and at night   you
are   close to the sky when the

moon shines through   the screen
window   Damp needles and earth
rise like incense but   still
you don't see   the tops of
the trees   touch one another

Listen

If you walk north from the cottage
into deep woods
and happen to look up at just the right moment,
and if, when you look up there,
your heart is full of what you do not yet know,
then, perhaps, you may see the owl
crouched like a cat
in the fork of the tallest fir.

If you stand at the west window,
there may be a blue heron fishing
beside the bench at the pond.
If you decide to learn patience today
and wait with her, motionless, for the careless fish,
soon you will find your eyes piercing weed
as one shadowy carp slides below
and everything but its gliding flesh falls away.

The cedar tree close to the south window
is never still.
She shakes water from the tips of her fronds;
she drapes branches across the view;
but it is her trunk that has reassured me
morning after morning, its huge weight soaring,
its two perfect, female fissures
moist again with the secretions of the dew.

If you lie at night by the east windows
where the roof slopes down, and if
your heart is full of what you might one day know,
you will hear the oak beams sing.
For seven years the sap will move
as the wood, lovingly shaped to its new task,
sings of the forest it left behind. If you listen,
you will learn there is no such thing as leaving.

Notes

FIESTA MAYOR, 1987

Fiesta Mayor is the major festival of the year. In Spain, each city, town and village has its own fiesta. The *ayuntamiento* is the town hall. *Cante hondo* is flamenco singing from Andalusia. *Turrón* is candy made from almonds and honey. A *purrón* is a vessel made of leather with a spout for drinking wine. A *paseo* is a walk. It often refers to the stroll before dinner. The *Guardias* are the civil guards who were greatly feared in Franco's time. A *maricón* is a gay man, a faggot.

RIGHT AT THE END OF EL PEÑON

El Peñon means a huge rock. In this case it is more like an island, just off the beach at Salobreña in southern Spain.

THE HIGH VILLAGES

The Alpujarras are part of the Sierra Nevada mountain range south of Granada, Spain.

LETTERS FROM EASTERN OREGON

The Umatilla Army Depot, just outside Hermiston, Oregon, was, in 1986, the second largest storage site for chemical weapons in the United States. In Catalonia, the *tramontana* is a strong wind that blows south from the Pyrenees.

About the Author

Judith Barrington was born in 1944 in Brighton, England. She lived in Spain from 1964 to 1966 and moved to Portland, Oregon in 1976. She has been a freelance writer, contributing columns on women's issues to newspapers nationwide, and book reviews to the feminist and mainstream media. She has taught Women's Studies at Portland State University, and currently teaches creative writing at Marylhurst College and at the Northwest Writing Institute at Lewis and Clark College. For part of each year, she teaches in the Arts in Education program. She is the founder of *Flight of the Mind*, a week-long summer writing workshop for women in the Oregon Cascades, at which she has taught the poetry section for the past five years. Her first book of poems, *Trying to be an Honest Woman* was published in 1985 by The Eighth Mountain Press

Marcia Barrentine designed the cover and created the cover art for *History and Geography*. She is a graphic designer and artist who lives in Portland, Oregon.

The cover typography and the text of this book were composed in a digitized version of Palatino. The book was printed and bound by McNaughton & Gunn Lithographers, Ann Arbor, Michigan, on acid-free paper.

History and Geography has been issued in a first edition of three thousand copies, of which twenty-five hundred are in paper and five hundred are in cloth.